# Methanol as a Marine Fuel: A Comprehensive Guide

**Contents**

Preface

Introduction

Prelude

Chapter 1: The Chemistry of Methanol

Chapter 2: Methanol's Advantages as a Marine Fuel

Chapter 3: Challenges of Using Methanol

Chapter 4: Methanol in Comparison with Other Alternative Marine Fuels

Chapter 5: Technological Aspects of Methanol Engines

Chapter 6: Regulatory and Compliance Landscape

Chapter 7: Case Studies: Methanol Adoption in the Maritime Industry

Chapter 8: Future Outlook for Methanol as a Marine Fuel

Conclusion

Appendixes

# Preface

As the shipping industry seeks alternative fuel solutions to meet decarbonization goals, methanol has emerged as a promising option for reducing greenhouse gas emissions and improving fuel efficiency. Methanol is not only abundant and widely available, but it also offers a cleaner-burning alternative to conventional marine fuels. With growing investments in methanol infrastructure and technologies, understanding its role in maritime operations has never been more critical.

*Methanol as a Marine Fuel: A Comprehensive Guide* is designed to equip maritime professionals with the knowledge needed to navigate this emerging fuel option. As part of the Gosships Learning Series, this book covers the fundamentals of methanol production, its environmental benefits, and the infrastructure required to incorporate methanol into modern shipping fleets. With real-world case studies and insights into regulatory compliance, this guide provides practical information for both industry veterans and those new to alternative marine fuels.

By completing this book, you will gain valuable knowledge on methanol's potential to help the maritime industry meet the challenges of stricter environmental regulations while remaining competitive in the global market. Each chapter is designed to not only provide theoretical understanding but also practical applications for implementing methanol as a marine fuel.

We hope this guide will enhance your understanding of methanol's future in shipping and support your professional development in this evolving sector.

# Introduction

Welcome to *Methanol as a Marine Fuel: A Comprehensive Guide*, part of the Gosships Learning Series, designed to provide maritime professionals with a detailed understanding of the opportunities and challenges associated with methanol as a marine fuel. As international shipping faces increasing pressure to reduce carbon emissions and transition to cleaner fuel alternatives, methanol stands out due to its lower emissions profile, scalability, and potential for renewable production.

This book will cover:

- **Methanol Production and Supply Chain**: Learn about how methanol is produced and transported, and explore the logistics of its supply chain.

- **Methanol's Role in Decarbonizing Shipping**: Understand how methanol compares to other alternative fuels in terms of reducing emissions and meeting regulatory requirements.

- **Infrastructure Requirements**: Dive into the storage, handling, and bunkering infrastructure needed for widespread methanol adoption in maritime operations.

- **Economic Considerations**: Explore the market viability of methanol as a marine fuel, including cost factors, global supply, and future demand trends.

- **Safety and Risk Management**: Learn the best practices for safely handling, storing, and using methanol in marine engines, along with regulatory frameworks to ensure compliance.

Upon completing this book, you will have the opportunity to test your knowledge through a certification exam. Successful completion will earn you a Certificate of Achievement, validating your expertise in this critical area of marine fuel innovation.

## Who is this book for?

This book is designed for:

- Ship operators, engineers, and fuel managers looking to adopt or transition to methanol as a marine fuel.

- Maritime professionals aiming to deepen their understanding of alternative fuels and compliance with new emissions regulations.

- Students and aspiring maritime personnel eager to gain a solid foundation in emerging fuel technologies.

- Regulatory and government personnel focused on developing policies for alternative fuel adoption and sustainability in the maritime industry.

By mastering the concepts in this book, you will be well-equipped to contribute to the transition toward cleaner fuels in shipping and drive innovation within your organization or sector.

# Gosships Learning Series 2024/2025

1. Hydrogen: The Fuel of the Future
2. Green Ammonia: The Next Big Thing in Shipping
3. Decarbonizing Shipping: Pathways to Zero Emissions
4. Battery Technology for Industrial Applications
5. Carbon Capture and Storage: Can It Save the Planet?
6. Biofuels 101: Turning Waste into Energy
7. Understanding LNG (Liquefied Natural Gas)
8. Methanol as a Marine Fuel
9. Offshore Wind Energy: The Future of Renewable Power
10. Tidal and Wave Energy: Harnessing the Ocean
11. Electrofuels: The Next Generation of Carbon-Neutral Fuels
12. Energy Storage Systems for Grid Reliability
13. Hydrogen Fuel Cells for Transportation
14. Solar Energy Innovations: Beyond Solar Panels
15. Smart Grids: The Backbone of Future Energy Systems
16. Ammonia-Hydrogen Blends: A Dual Fuel Solution?
17. Nuclear Power: Small Modular Reactors for a Low-Carbon Future
18. Hydropower: The Oldest Renewable Energy Source
19. Decentralized Energy Systems: Microgrids for Resilience
20. Energy Efficiency Technologies for Industry
21. Hydrogen Production from Seawater
22. Fuel Cells for Maritime Applications
23. Geothermal Energy: Unlocking Earth's Heat
24. Future of EV Charging Infrastructure

25. Synthetic Fuels: Bridging the Gap to Decarbonization
26. Cybersecurity for Maritime and Offshore Operations
27. AI and Automation in Shipping and Logistics
28. Digital Twins in Maritime: Revolutionizing Asset Management
29. Risk Management in Offshore and Maritime Operations
30. Compliance with IMO 2020 Regulations
31. Sustainable Ship Design: Reducing Environmental Impact
32. Marine Renewable Energy: Wave, Tidal, and Offshore Wind Integration
33. Ballast Water Management Systems
34. Blockchain Technology in Shipping: Improving Transparency & Efficiency
35. Effective Supply Chain Management for Energy Industries
36. Leadership in the Energy Transition
37. Effective Crisis Management in Maritime Operations
38. Shipyard Safety Management Systems
39. Port State Control (PSC) Inspection Readiness
40. Remote Vessel Operations and Autonomous Shipping
41. Optimizing Fleet Performance with Data Analytics
42. Maritime Environmental Regulations: Staying Ahead of Compliance
43. Advanced Maintenance Strategies: Condition Monitoring & Predictive Maintenance
44. Global LNG Market: Trends and Opportunities
45. Incident Investigation in Maritime Operations
46. International Maritime Law: Key Concepts and Applications
47. Emergency Preparedness and Response for Offshore Oil & Gas

48. **Energy Transition Strategies for Oil and Gas Companies**

49. **Maritime Drones: Applications and Safety Considerations**

50. **Effective Project Management in Offshore Energy Projects**

**All Rights Reserved Disclaimer**

The contents of this book, including but not limited to all text, graphics, images, logos, and designs, are the intellectual property of Gosships LLC and are protected by copyright law. No part of this publication may be reproduced, distributed, transmitted, displayed, or modified in any form or by any means, including photocopying, recording, or other electronic or mechanical methods, without the prior written permission of the publisher, except in the case of brief quotations in critical reviews or articles.

The information contained within this book is for educational purposes only and is provided "as is" without warranty of any kind, either expressed or implied. The authors and publishers disclaim any liability for any direct, indirect, or consequential loss or damage arising from the use of the material in this book.

For permissions or inquiries, please contact: admin@gosships.com

© 2024 Gosships LLC. All rights reserved.

# Prelude

Methanol is gaining momentum as a marine fuel due to its environmental benefits and growing alignment with global emissions regulations. This guide will provide an overview of methanol as a viable alternative to traditional marine fuels like heavy fuel oil (HFO) and marine gas oil (MGO). As the maritime industry faces increasing pressure to reduce carbon emissions, methanol offers a bridge to cleaner, more sustainable shipping.

In this guide, we'll explore methanol's chemistry, its benefits and challenges, comparisons with other fuels, the technical considerations for engines, and real-world examples of adoption. Whether you are a shipowner, operator, or industry stakeholder, understanding methanol can help inform decisions on compliance, retrofits, and the future of your fleet.

# Chapter 1
# The Chemistry of Methanol

Methanol, also known as wood alcohol, is one of the simplest alcohols, with the chemical formula $CH_3OH$. It is a clear, colorless liquid that is both flammable and toxic. Despite these properties, methanol's low carbon content makes it a promising alternative for marine fuel, as it releases lower $CO_2$ emissions when burned compared to fossil fuels like diesel or HFO.

## Production of Methanol

Methanol is traditionally produced from natural gas via reforming processes, but it can also be made from renewable sources, such as biomass, or through carbon capture and recycling methods. This gives methanol the potential to be a carbon-neutral fuel, especially when synthesized using green energy or renewable feedstocks.

## Storage and Handling Considerations

Methanol is relatively easy to store and transport compared to gases like LNG (liquefied natural gas). It remains liquid at ambient temperatures and can be handled similarly to existing liquid fuels. However, safety protocols must be strictly followed, as methanol is toxic if ingested and highly flammable. Proper storage involves using corrosion-resistant materials, as methanol can be corrosive to some metals.

# Chapter 2
# Methanol's Advantages as a Marine Fuel

## Environmental Benefits

One of the key drivers for methanol adoption is its environmental performance. Unlike heavy fuel oil, methanol produces no sulfur emissions, making it compliant with International Maritime Organization (IMO) regulations for sulfur caps. Additionally, it burns cleaner than conventional marine fuels, reducing particulate matter and $NO_x$ emissions, which are harmful to both human health and the environment.

Methanol also provides a pathway to reducing greenhouse gas emissions. While burning methanol still releases $CO_2$, it produces 25% less $CO_2$ compared to conventional fuels. If produced from renewable sources, methanol can be nearly carbon-neutral, helping the shipping industry meet its long-term decarbonization goals.

## Operational Benefits

Methanol can be stored in existing liquid fuel tanks, which simplifies the transition process. Retrofitting existing engines to use methanol is also relatively straightforward and cost-effective, making it an attractive option for shipowners who want to reduce emissions without fully replacing their fleet.

## Retrofit Potential

Methanol can be used in both new builds and retrofitted vessels. Retrofitting a ship to run on methanol involves installing new fuel injection systems but is generally simpler than converting to LNG or hydrogen. The availability of dual-fuel engines, which can run on both methanol and conventional fuels, offers flexibility for ship operators transitioning to greener fuels.

# Chapter 3
# Challenges of Using Methanol

## Energy Density

One of the challenges of using methanol is its lower energy density compared to traditional marine fuels. Methanol has about half the energy content of diesel per unit volume, meaning ships need to carry roughly twice as much fuel to cover the same distance. This can affect fuel storage requirements and reduce available cargo space.

## Cost Considerations

Methanol prices vary depending on production methods. Conventionally produced methanol from natural gas is currently more expensive than HFO but cheaper than LNG. However, renewable methanol is still relatively costly, though prices are expected to decrease as production scales up and carbon pricing mechanisms come into play.

## Infrastructure Limitations

While methanol can be stored in liquid tanks, global infrastructure for methanol bunkering is still underdeveloped compared to more established fuels like LNG. However, ports are beginning to adapt as demand for alternative fuels grows, and investments in methanol bunkering facilities are expected to increase over time.

## Safety and Regulatory Concerns

Methanol is toxic and can be absorbed through the skin or ingested, requiring strict handling protocols. It is also highly flammable, although its behavior is more predictable and manageable than LNG. Shipowners and crews need to undergo proper training in methanol handling to mitigate risks.

# Chapter 4

# Methanol in Comparison with Other Alternative Marine Fuels

### LNG vs. Methanol

LNG has higher energy density and emits fewer greenhouse gases compared to HFO, but its infrastructure is costly and complex due to the need for cryogenic storage. Methanol, in contrast, can be stored at ambient temperatures and does not require the same level of infrastructure investment. Both fuels have the potential to lower emissions, but methanol may offer an easier and more cost-effective transition for shipowners.

### Ammonia vs. Methanol

Ammonia is another alternative fuel gaining attention due to its zero-carbon emissions when burned. However, ammonia is toxic and has handling challenges, as it is highly corrosive and requires careful storage. Methanol, while not carbon-free, has a more established supply chain and fewer safety concerns.

### Hydrogen vs. Methanol

Hydrogen is often viewed as the ultimate solution for zero-emission shipping, but its storage and handling are more challenging due to its low energy density and the need for pressurized or cryogenic tanks. Methanol, on the other hand, offers an easier-to-implement solution, even though it is not entirely emissions-free.

# Chapter 5
# Technological Aspects of Methanol Engines

## Methanol-Ready Engines

Several engine manufacturers have developed methanol-ready engines, which are optimized for dual-fuel operation, allowing ships to run on both methanol and traditional fuels. These engines have been designed to meet the demands of modern shipping, balancing emissions reduction with fuel efficiency.

## Engine Conversion

Converting a conventional diesel engine to run on methanol involves modifications to the fuel injection system and storage tanks. These conversions are cost-effective compared to LNG retrofits, making methanol an appealing option for shipowners looking to minimize capital expenditures.

## Efficiency Considerations

Methanol engines tend to have slightly lower thermal efficiency compared to diesel engines, but they still offer competitive fuel performance. The fuel consumption rate may be higher due to methanol's lower energy density, but this can be managed through optimized engine design and operational practices.

# Chapter 6
# Regulatory and Compliance Landscape

## International Maritime Organization (IMO) Regulations

Methanol is an attractive option for compliance with IMO regulations, including the 2020 sulfur cap and future greenhouse gas reduction targets for 2050. Methanol's sulfur-free combustion and lower $CO_2$ emissions make it a compliant fuel for shipping companies looking to stay ahead of regulatory changes.

## Flag State and Port State Control

As with all fuels, methanol requires compliance with flag state and port state control regulations. These regulations ensure that methanol-powered vessels meet safety, environmental, and operational standards set by maritime authorities worldwide.

## Methanol Bunkering Standards

Emerging global standards for methanol bunkering are being developed to ensure safe and efficient fuel transfer. Ports and operators must follow strict procedures to prevent spills, leaks, and other hazards associated with methanol fueling.

# Chapter 7

# Case Studies: Methanol Adoption in the Maritime Industry

## Stena Line's Methanol-Powered Ferry

Stena Line's conversion of its ferry Stena Germanica to run on methanol was a pioneering move. The retrofit was completed in 2015, and the ferry has since demonstrated the viability of methanol as a marine fuel, achieving significant reductions in emissions while maintaining operational efficiency.

## Waterfront Shipping's Methanol-Fueled Fleet

Waterfront Shipping, a division of Methanex, operates a fleet of methanol-powered vessels, proving the scalability of methanol as a marine fuel. Their fleet, including dual-fuel tankers, has shown strong performance in terms of both emissions reduction and operational reliability.

## Maersk's Methanol Strategy

Maersk, one of the world's largest shipping companies, has committed to using methanol as part of its strategy to decarbonize its fleet. Maersk's order for methanol-powered containerships highlights the growing industry shift toward cleaner fuels.

# Chapter 8

# Future Outlook for Methanol as a Marine Fuel

## Technological Innovation and Research

Ongoing research in methanol production, engine technology, and emissions reduction is driving methanol's potential as a marine fuel. Advances in renewable methanol production and carbon capture technologies could significantly reduce the lifecycle emissions of methanol, making it an even more attractive option.

## Investment in Infrastructure

As the demand for alternative fuels grows, ports and bunkering companies are beginning to invest in methanol infrastructure. This will help support the widespread adoption of methanol as a marine fuel and ensure a reliable supply chain for shipowners.

## Role in Decarbonization

Methanol's role in decarbonizing the shipping industry is likely to grow as regulatory pressure increases. While not the only solution, methanol is well-positioned to be part of the future fuel mix, especially as renewable methanol production becomes more affordable and widespread.

## Conclusion

Methanol represents a practical, scalable solution for shipowners looking to reduce emissions and comply with stricter environmental regulations. Its environmental benefits, combined with relatively straightforward retrofitting processes, make it an appealing alternative to LNG and other fuels. Although challenges remain—particularly with energy density and infrastructure—methanol's potential in helping the maritime industry achieve its sustainability goals is significant.

For shipowners and operators, methanol offers an opportunity to transition toward greener shipping without the need for massive overhauls of existing fleets. With growing investment in methanol-ready engines and bunkering facilities, methanol is set to play a key role in the future of maritime fuel.

# Appendix

- **Glossary of Key Terms**
- **List of Major Producers and Suppliers of Methanol**
- **References and Further Reading**

## Appendix 1: Glossary of Key Terms

1. **Additive**: A substance added to methanol to enhance performance or stability in fuel applications.

2. **Air Emissions**: Pollutants released into the atmosphere from combustion engines using methanol as fuel.

3. **Alternative Fuel**: A fuel other than traditional petroleum-based fuels, such as methanol, used in maritime operations.

4. **Bio-Methanol**: Methanol produced from renewable sources like biomass, offering a carbon-neutral alternative to fossil-based methanol.

5. **Blending**: The process of mixing methanol with other fuels to create a hybrid fuel for marine engines.

6. **Bunkering**: The process of refueling a ship with methanol, which includes the infrastructure and logistics for safe fuel transfer.

7. **Carbon Dioxide ($CO_2$)**: A greenhouse gas produced by burning fuels, including methanol; its reduction is a goal for decarbonizing shipping.

8. **Carbon Intensity**: The amount of $CO_2$ emissions produced per unit of energy, used to measure the environmental impact of methanol as a fuel.

9. **Carbon Neutral**: A state where carbon emissions are balanced by carbon removal, making bio-methanol an attractive option for marine fuel.

10. **Catalyst**: A substance that speeds up chemical reactions, used in methanol production processes like reforming or synthesis.

11. **Combustion**: The process of burning methanol in an engine to produce power, releasing heat and exhaust gases.

12. **Decarbonization**: The process of reducing carbon emissions in shipping by switching to alternative fuels like methanol.

13. **Density**: The mass of methanol per unit volume, important for calculating fuel storage and energy content.

14. **Dual-Fuel Engine**: A marine engine capable of running on both methanol and conventional fuels like diesel or LNG.

15. **ECA (Emission Control Area)**: Designated maritime areas where stricter emission standards apply, promoting the use of cleaner fuels like methanol.

16. **Emission Reduction**: The decrease of pollutants, including $CO_2$ and $NO_x$, achieved by using methanol instead of traditional fuels.

17. **Energy Density**: The amount of energy stored in methanol per unit of volume, lower than traditional fuels but sufficient for marine use.

18. **Exhaust Gas**: The gases emitted by a ship's engine after methanol combustion, containing pollutants and greenhouse gases.

19. **Feedstock**: The raw materials used to produce methanol, including natural gas, coal, or renewable biomass.

20. **Flash Point**: The lowest temperature at which methanol vapor can ignite, important for assessing fuel safety.

21. **GHG (Greenhouse Gas)**: Gases like $CO_2$ and methane that trap heat in the atmosphere, contributing to climate change.

22. **Hydrogen**: A component used in methanol production and a potential future marine fuel in combination with methanol.

23. **IMO (International Maritime Organization)**: The UN agency responsible for regulating international shipping, including fuel standards like those for methanol.

24. **Infrastructure**: The physical facilities needed for methanol production, storage, and bunkering in the maritime industry.

25. **Internal Combustion Engine**: An engine that burns fuel, including methanol, to produce power for ship propulsion.

26. **LHV (Lower Heating Value)**: The amount of heat released by burning methanol, used to compare its energy content with other fuels.

27. **Liquefied Natural Gas (LNG)**: A competing alternative marine fuel, often compared to methanol in terms of emissions and infrastructure.

28. **Methanol**: A simple alcohol-based fuel used as an alternative to traditional marine fuels, offering lower emissions.

29. **Methanol Synthesis**: The chemical process used to produce methanol from natural gas, coal, or biomass.

30. **$NO_x$ (Nitrogen Oxides)**: Harmful emissions produced during the combustion of fuel, including methanol, but at lower levels than traditional fuels.

31. **Particulate Matter (PM)**: Small particles emitted during fuel combustion, which methanol helps reduce compared to heavy fuels.

32. **Pilot Fuel**: A small amount of conventional fuel used to initiate combustion in a dual-fuel engine running on methanol.

33. **Port State Control (PSC)**: The inspection of ships by local authorities to ensure compliance with international regulations, including those related to methanol use.

34. **Primary Fuel**: The main fuel used in a marine engine, such as methanol when running on alternative fuels.

35. **Renewable Methanol**: Methanol produced from renewable sources like biomass or $CO_2$ capture, offering sustainable marine fuel solutions.

36. **Retrofit**: The modification of existing ships to enable them to run on methanol, rather than traditional marine fuels.

37. **Safety Regulations**: Guidelines governing the safe handling, storage, and use of methanol as a marine fuel.

38. **Self-Ignition Temperature**: The temperature at which methanol ignites without an external flame, lower than that of diesel.

39. **Ship-to-Ship Transfer**: The process of transferring methanol fuel between vessels at sea, requiring specialized equipment and safety protocols.

40. **$SO_x$ (Sulfur Oxides)**: Pollutants produced from burning sulfur-containing fuels, significantly reduced when using methanol.

41. **Solubility**: The ability of methanol to dissolve in water, which impacts its environmental behavior in case of spills.

42. **Storage Tank**: A cryogenic or pressurized container used to store methanol on ships or at bunkering terminals.

43. **Sulfur-Free Fuel**: A characteristic of methanol that eliminates sulfur oxide emissions, helping ships comply with stricter environmental regulations.

44. **Sustainability**: The environmental and economic viability of using methanol as a marine fuel, particularly when sourced from renewable materials.

45. **Tank Barge**: A specialized vessel used to transport methanol fuel, often to offshore or remote locations.

46. **Tanker Ship**: A large ship designed to transport bulk liquids, including methanol, across long distances.

47. **Toxicity**: The degree to which methanol can harm humans or marine life if ingested or inhaled.

48. **Volatility**: The tendency of methanol to evaporate quickly at room temperature, a factor in its storage and handling.

49. **Wobbe Index**: A measure used to compare the energy output of different fuels, including methanol, when burned in an engine.

50. **Zero-Emission Fuel**: A fuel that produces no greenhouse gases during combustion, a target for future marine fuels, including methanol.

## Appendix 2: List of Major Producers and Suppliers of Methanol

1. **Methanex Corporation**
    - Location: Global (Headquarters: Vancouver, Canada)
    - Overview: The world's largest producer and supplier of methanol. Operates production sites in North and South America, Asia, and Europe.
    - Website: www.methanex.com

2. **Proman**
    - Location: Switzerland
    - Overview: A major player in the methanol industry, focusing on petrochemical production. Proman operates facilities in Trinidad, the U.S., and Oman.
    - Website: www.proman.org

3. **OCI N.V.**
    - Location: Netherlands
    - Overview: A leading global producer of methanol, ammonia, and other chemicals. Operates methanol plants

in the U.S. and the Netherlands.

- Website: www.oci.nl

4. **SABIC**

    - Location: Saudi Arabia
    - Overview: A major global chemical producer, including methanol. SABIC is one of the largest methanol producers in the Middle East.
    - Website: www.sabic.com

5. **Zagros Petrochemical Company**

    - Location: Iran
    - Overview: One of the largest methanol producers in the world, based in Iran, serving the global market with a significant focus on Asian buyers.
    - Website: www.zpcir.com

6. **Southern Chemical Corporation**

    - Location: USA
    - Overview: A key supplier of methanol in North and South America, sourcing methanol from Methanex and other producers.
    - Website: www.southernchemical.com

7. **Atlantic Methanol Production Company (AMPCO)**

    - Location: Equatorial Guinea
    - Overview: AMPCO operates one of the largest methanol production plants in Africa, supplying markets in the U.S. and Europe.
    - Website: www.ampcogeq.com

8. **China National Offshore Oil Corporation (CNOOC)**

    - Location: China

- Overview: CNOOC is a significant methanol producer in China, with extensive operations in methanol production and chemical supply.
- Website: www.cnooc.com.cn

9. **Petronas**
   - Location: Malaysia
   - Overview: Malaysia's national oil and gas company, producing methanol from its facilities in Sarawak. It's a major supplier to Southeast Asia.
   - Website: www.petronas.com

10. **Qatar Fuel Additives Company (QAFAC)**
    - Location: Qatar
    - Overview: A leading producer of methanol and MTBE (methyl tert-butyl ether), supplying the global market from its state-of-the-art plant in Mesaieed, Qatar.
    - Website: www.qafac.com.qa

# Appendix 3: References and Further Reading

1. **International Maritime Organization (IMO)**
   - IMO's regulatory framework on alternative fuels and emissions: www.imo.org

2. **Methanex Corporation: White Papers and Industry Reports**
   - Comprehensive industry research and insights on methanol as a marine fuel: www.methanex.com

3. **Proman: Methanol Sustainability Reports**
   - Environmental benefits of methanol and future fuel innovations: www.proman.org

4. **Lloyd's Register: Methanol as a Marine Fuel**

- In-depth technical papers and case studies on the use of methanol in the shipping industry: www.lr.org

5. **DNV GL: Alternative Fuels Insight Platform**
    - Data and analysis on methanol and other alternative marine fuels: www.dnv.com

6. **Maersk: Decarbonization Strategy**
    - Maersk's strategy and investments in methanol-powered vessels: www.maersk.com

7. **Stena Line: Methanol Pilot Projects**
    - Case study on Stena Line's methanol-powered ferry conversion: www.stenaline.com

8. **Waterfront Shipping: Methanol Fleet Performance**
    - Reports on Waterfront Shipping's methanol-fueled vessels: www.waterfront-shipping.com

9. **The Methanol Institute**
    - Global trade association for the methanol industry, providing comprehensive resources on methanol's use as a marine fuel: www.methanol.org

10. **American Bureau of Shipping (ABS)**
    - Insights and guidelines for methanol bunkering and ship design: www.eagle.org

www.ingramcontent.com/pod-product-compliance
Lightning Source LLC
Chambersburg PA
CBHW051533240526
45471CB00019B/1339